Book of Parables III

Divine Lessons #36-42 from "Thy Kingdom Come"

BRIAN SMITH

Copyright © 2019 by Brian Smith, DDS Publishing

1st Edition

This is a work of Christian apologetics. Names, characters, places and incidents are either the product of the author's imagination or are used fictionally. Any resemblance to actual persons or organizations, living or dead, is entirely coincidental.

No part of this book may be reproduced in any manner whatsoever without written permission, except in the case of brief quotations embodied in the critical articles and reviews.

Printed and bound in the USA.

Cover design, symbols, characters, names, music, artwork, interior layout, and print are all copyright protected.

ISBN: 978-0-9991641-5-0

Introduction

Book of Parables III is the sixth book written in the series "Thy Kingdom Come". This book was written to be a companion aid to your personal Bible study and growth. The series was not written to take the place, nor over-shadow, nor lessen any of parabolic messages taught by Jesus Christ. Only Jesus can teach true parables, forgive personal sin, purify the soul, perform heavenly miracles, heal the sick, and also raise Himself from the dead. No mortal can do any these things, only He can.

Book of Parables III was written with the intention to bring additional emphasis to the lost and broken, the saved vs. the unsaved, and all who have not sought in earnest wisdom and enlightenment from the Parables which Jesus Christ taught. May you, the reader, receive many blessings from the Book of Parables, inspired from the wisdom and teachings of the Holy Scriptures, which will bring you closer to eternal salvation, forgiveness, peace, happiness, and joy; also, that you also might better walk in God's Light forever, and inherit Eternal Life under His care with His boundless love, grace, mercy and hope ever-lasting…

This book was primarily written to help the beginner student of the Bible understand the unified message of the Triune God (The Father, Jesus Christ The Son, and The Holy Ghost: aka The Divine Comforter, Counselor, Helper, Companion, Advocate, Paraclete, Melitz Yosher, & Ruach ha-Kodesh) which exist All-as-One-in-the-Same as The Creators of Mankind, but live in three different worlds of different dimensions all-at-the-same-time. Different theologians through the years have given us different interpretations with different translations of the scripture for us to unravel which can cause confusion. For example, in the Lord's Prayer, the Book of Mathew in the New International Version reads as follows, "And forgive us our debts, as we also have forgiven our debtors."[1] The translated word debt, the author believes refers to the First World of flesh and earth, the world of Jesus Christ, and the world we sojourn in. This is world of material things like skin, wood, paper, iron, wool, water, salt, and myrrh. Debt is created and loaned in the world to a person of a specific sojourn, being all of the first world (earth, ground, man, etc…). This thing of debt has defined borders, boundaries and consequences, all of which are inherently tangible, and finite. In other versions of the Bible, the same scripture reads, "And forgive us our trespasses, as we also forgive those which trespass against us."[2] The word trespass, the author believes refers to the spiritual world, the Invisible World of the Holy Spirit, also meaning The World of Spiritual Invisible Warfare in which man is alien[3] to. The act of spiritual (as well as mental) trespassing does not going across a border or physical boundary which is tangible, but means to trespass into another space un-invited or unrightfully[4], thereby taking what is perceived as theirs via God given rights (which is unjustly and erroneously perceived), but altogether having no real tangible finite value other than pride, curiosity, or seeking self-awareness, therefore being much less describable to a mortal's mind or comprehension, so is put under the jurisdiction of the Holy Spirit, a.k.a. Great Counselor[5] and Comforter of the world, who has been placed as The Domino to assist man into making correct and true decisions which help guide him into a Godly (pure) life, then receive salvation through grace, while serving others, helping the world, and doing no harm to himself.

And in another interpretation of the scripture the same scripture reads, "and forgive us our sins, that we also forgive those

---

[1] Matthew 6:12 (NASB: New American Standard Bible)
[2] Matthew 6:12 (NMB: New Matthew Bible)
[3] Psalm 146:9, I Peter 2:11
[4] Romans 5:12-21 (NIV: New International Version)
[5] John 14:26 (CSB: Christian Standard Bible)

who sin against us."[6] *The author believes that this term (sin) refers to the laws governing the third Holy world, aka Heaven and the world of God Our Father, as well as our Creator, the 'One-who-lives-in-Heaven-with-His-Son', whom therein both are perfect without possession of any sin. Because the word "sin" is used synonymously to mean imperfection, then all the mirrored forms, versions, and uses fall under and remain inclusive below this use. Therefore, this Holy and universal version with inference of the third world of Heaven is used in reference to the highest order of being, the third world of the Triune Godhead, the term which encumbers and encapsulates all other versions and uses under it. Jesus referred to himself as The Son of His Father in Heaven (Who had been sent), regarding His position many times, giving all subordination to His Father God, when saying it was not He who made decisions for man on earth but only His Father in Heaven.*[7] *And He had been given the authority and reserved this authority to make all final decisions for man later after His ascension to His throne at the side of His Father in Heaven.*[8]

So, while reading through Book of Parables III, your enlightened journey will prayerfully be assisted in a higher understanding of the different enlightenments of the Triune God knowing that man's lives have multiple components of knowledge which are woven into three parts: the material, spiritual, and Heavenly; all of which overlap into one beautiful mosaic of a single entity in uniqueness we call us…. From creation, to birth, to death, and then back to life. Our unique legacies as we know them now, are a journey of faith and hope and being tested, going from the finite and the tangible, traveling towards the infinite and the intangible, to being understood as the ultimate life everlasting for

---

[6] Matthew 6:12 (EXB: Expanded Bible, TLB: The Living Bible)
[7] Matthew 6:10 (NIV: New International Version)
[8] Revelation 19:12-16 (NIV: New International Version as witnessed by John)

those who are The Believers in the understanding of the Triune God, and also in Jesus Christ who was sent to die, rise from the grave, and then live again to show us the way.[9]

The Apostle Paul wrote in 53 AD... that everyone...Hebrew and Greek, Gentile and Jew, are all alike who live under the law. He wrote attesting that---

We are all alike because The Holy Spirit said:

"There is no one righteous, not even one;

there is no one who understands, non-one who purposely seeks God."

"All have turned away, they have together become worthless, and there is no one who does good, not even one."

"Their throats are open graves, their tongues practice deceit."

"The poison of vipers is on their lips."

"Their mouths are full of cursing and bitterness."

"Their feet are swift to shed blood; ruin and mark misery their ways, and they way of peace they do not know."

"There is no fear of God before their ways."

So, continuing...Paul wrote: "Now we know that whatever the law says, it says to those under the law so that every mouth may be silenced, and the whole world be held accountable to God. Therefore, no-one will be declared righteous in His sight by

---

[9] John 11: 25-26, Hebrews 13:20-21 (KJV: King James Version)

observing the law, rather by observing the law, we become conscious of our sin."

    Romans 3:10-20

Book of Parables III (36-41)

Introduction iv

The Good Husband & Wife 1

The Three Halos & Wedding 4

The Greatest Word 8

The First Right of all Rights 12

Pompous-Ass Mercury 13

The Only Standard 17

If You Love Me 20

Divine Lesson #36

The Good Husband & Wife

An angel went to the Lord God and asked Him, "Why do you make mankind live, breathe, and cherish You[10] as good husbands and wives[11]. Is this marital union not created the same as the animals of the fields, the birds of the air, or the insects of the swamps?"[12]

Then, the Lord God replied, "Iron sharpens iron![13] With the animals of the fields, the birds of the air, and the insects of the swamps, I did not give them a covenant[14], but with mankind I did. For this reason, I have raised him up and given man a soul, and given him dominion over the earth[15]. The birds of the air, the animals of the field, and the insects of the swamps, I saved them all two by two[16] just the same when I destroyed the earth, but to man I saved him more[17] to gave him direction[18], with thought

---

[10] I Peter 2:9
[11] Genesis 2:24,
[12] Leviticus 22:19
[13] Proverbs 27:17
[14] John 5: 24
[15] Genesis 1:26, 9:2-3
[16] Genesis 6:19
[17] Genesis 6:18
[18] Genesis 9:5

and choice[19], so that he might multiply two by two, forsaking all others[20], each as husband and wife[21], so that one day I might dine with them later and they with me in a communion as a covenant which is more than a contract.[22] Because of this, I sent my Son, as my blood covenant[23], in Whom I am well pleased[24], to join with them and be more than a contract, to be loved and cherished and to give Eternal Life[25], that all might dine and live in purity[26] together eternally. With the birds of the air, the animals of the field, and the insects of the swamp, I have made no such covenant, and I make no promise. I do not promise them anything more than to be, but good stewards of what I have given to them[27], the same which I have asked of man. But, when man acts just as animals of the field, and birds of the air, and insects of the swamp, and continuously commits sins for which he is not sorry nor repents, then he will be disqualified and lose My covenant and I shall remove from him My offer of eternal life[28]. For if any man so loves the things of the world or anything more than Me, he is not worthy of Me[29].

I tell you the Truth, the world will be judged for all choices of insolence in its final days[30], and for what it has

---

[19] Isaiah 55:8
[20] Philippians 3:7-8
[21] I Corinthians 7:14
[22] Proverb 23:1, John 6:46-51
[23] I Corinthians 10:16, John 6:53-59
[24] Luke 3:22
[25] John 10:25-30
[26] John 3:15
[27] Genesis 9:5
[28] I Corinthians 9:27, Ephesians 5:3-5, I Corinthians 6:9, Galatians 5:19-21, Revelations 21:6-8
[29] Matthew 10:37
[30] John 16:11, Romans 6:19-20

loved and it has not loved, and everything in it will be consumed by My hand of fire (and basalt) because of him who did not love and serve Me First[31]; and all shall be separated into sheep and goats[32] by their first loves. For I did not come to bring peace, but I came to separate father from son, mother from daughter, and brother from brother, that all might know who loves me first and keeps My commands[33] more than the birds of the air, the animals of the fields, and the insects of the swamps. To all, I keep my covenant and my promises[34]. And to those, who remain un-cleaved as good husbands and wives and who are faithful in the covenant of marriage, I will love them more for their faithfulness as they become more sharpened and more Holy in My name; just as I am faithful and sharpened to them, for they will be truly blessed, just as, My earthly parents, Mary and Joseph, who are blessed because they suffered well[35] to keep My covenant[36]; and these shall be known as those who chose to die to self, putting each other first, and inheriting My eternal love.[37]" Amen

---

[31] John 3:36
[32] Matthew 25:31-46
[33] Matthew 10:24
[34] Matthew 11:28-29, 2 Peter 1:4, 2 Corinthians 1:20
[35] Galatians 4:19
[36] Luke 2:39-40
[37] Matthew 5:5

-- Book of Parables III --

Divine Lesson #37

The Three Halos & Wedding

An angel asked the Lord God, creator of Heavens and Earth, "Where is home[38] for us, for we are constantly moved to and fro from this world to the next?"

The Lord God looked around and gazed into the stars and then to the saints in Heaven which surrounded Him before responding, and then He said, "Where ever I am… there are you also.[39] You are my celestial beings which have been given one Halo, and one covenant, one oath, and but one wedding all at one time. But man has been given these same things in three parts, for these things live and breathe in multiple dimensions.[40]"

The angel then asked this after receiving this divine answer, "So, why then does man receive his in three parts?[41] We have no way to discern this logic. We know nothing more than just to rise and to respond, at the call of Your will."

---

[38] Ecclesiastes 12:5
[39] Genesis 28:15
[40] Matthew 28:19
[41] Luke 3:16

The Lord God, looked at the angel and smiled upon His good and faithful servant.[42] As He was preparing His answer (which took many years to prepare and cleanse the earth), The Lord God called The Holy Spirit[43] and His Son, Jesus[44], to be next to Him at His side when He answered. Then the Three spoke together to the Heavens in unison saying, "In the beginning, We Were[45] and We created the heavens and the earth.[46] This did not happen by chaos, big bang or chance, nor evolve from the sea. We, as One, created you, My angels, and all the others, the whole world with its legends of mystery, and We also created the first man formed with a soul, Adam,[47] in our image[48]. To you, the angels, We gave one mind with one soul, to be spread amongst all of you, unified into one heart, but to man we gave to each his own.[49] And then to each man, beginning with the second Adam[50] We set aside three halos to be claimed[51] to those who could pass the test with Our promise, then at a later time to wed if he is not distracted by the Evil One[52] (or the halos will be reclaimed)[53]: one halo for Me,[54] one for The Christ,[55] and one for the Holy Spirit.

---

[42] Hebrews 1:7
[43] John 14:26
[44] Luke 3:22
[45] Genesis 1:26
[46] Genesis 1:1
[47] Genesis 2:7
[48] Genesis 1:27
[49] Genesis 2:16-17
[50] Romans 5:12-21
[51] Romans 6:17
[52] 1 John 5:19
[53] I Corinthians 9:27, Esther 7,8
[54] Luke 15:22
[55] Acts 24:5

When Man is found[56] he accepts Christ's proposal,[57] then he wears the first halo for his engagement;[58] when man is faithful,[59] obedient,[60] and abides in Me,[61] he wears the second halo, and he is wed with Me; and when this man suffers,[62] takes on the Holy things of burden and concern of his back looking then to the Holy Spirit for guidance,[63] and he makes his body his slave,[64] and grows in Our spirit and desires,[65] honoring the angels who have been sent to support him in his test,[66] and then finds the entrance to the narrow gate of heaven,[67] then he is awarded the third halo of eternal life. You My dear angel, have been awarded your eternal life for being My good and faithful servant,[68] a warrior[69] and a messenger[70] and also for not being distracted from your calling which would be caused by the Evil One and his band of lying followers, so you wear only one halo for your faithfulness; but for the righteous man[71], who is wedded and has a faithful heart, he or she is awarded all three. These shall be called every saint,[72] and receive Eternal Life[73] with a

---

[56] Matthew 7:7-8
[57] Romans 15:7
[58] Luke 7:50
[59] 2 Corinthians 2:9
[60] John 15:4
[61] Ephesians 5:22-33
[62] Job 36:15
[63] John 14:26
[64] I Corinthians 9:27
[65] I Peter 2:1-3
[66] Psalm 91:11, Luke 4:10
[67] Matthew &:13
[68] Matthew 18:10
[69] Judges 6:12
[70] Job 33:23
[71] I Timothy 6:11
[72] Daniel 7:18
[73] John 5:24

home very similar to yours.[74] There are many rooms where every saint and angel shall abide, shall live and be placed,[75] to be grouped into similar hearts of my adopted children and united into one mind and soul with the others. And then all the saints, but not all the angels, will wear many crowns.[76] Also, I tell you the truth here, that no one shall ever wear, adorn, nor touch My crown, nor look upon My Holy Face, without My consent first, but Me.[77]

---

[74] Ecclesiastes 12:5
[75] John 14:2
[76] James 1:12
[77] Revelation 14:14

-- Book of Parables III --

Divine Lesson #38

The Greatest Word

An angel stood before the Lord, looking up from Lower Paradise with wings out stretched and asked Him, "Lord, My Creator, of all the words which come from a man's mouth, which is the greatest word of them all? And, can man even possess such a great word since on his lips is the poison of vipers, with a mouth full of cursing and bitterness?"[78]

The Lord God, looked at Him in disbelief. Then the Lord said, "You were there as a seer when My son answered twice the question on how to receive Eternal Life. And what did He say?"

Then the angel responded, "The Christ[79] answered this way when asked… Sell all that you have, give it to the poor, then you will have treasure in Heaven. Then come and follow me, and then you will have eternal life.[80]

He then said, it is harder for a camel to go through the eye of a needle than it is for a rich man to get into Heaven.[81]"

---

[78] Romans 3:13-14
[79] Matthew 1:16, 16:16, 22:42, John 1:41, Acts 5:42, 9:22, 18:28, 26:23, Romans 6:4, 7:4, 8:17, 8:35, 10:4, 12:5, 15:3,
[80] Mark 10:21
[81] Mark 10:25

"This is true, My good and faithful servant. So, what did The Christ[82] say when was asked a second time?" demands the Lord God Almighty!

The angel quaked, and hesitated to make his humble reply. But the angel possessed only thoughts void of free will and free volition, so after pledging his loyalty solely to the Triune again, he was validated, convicted, bound and cleaved for His eternal destination once more, then answered, "The Christ answered the second time this way…Love the Lord your God with all your heart and with all your soul and with all your strength and with all your mind; and, also love your neighbor as yourself. [83] Do this and you will live.[84]"

"You have answered correctly," said the Lord God to the angel He so loved. "So, now you tell me what is the answer to your question…what is the greatest word man can speak?"

"I know but one answer which You gave by Your mouth when asked this question as well about whom shall inherit eternal life, and the answer You and I ask is found in Your own words, the angel said. "You told us that You so loved the world, that You gave Your only Son, Jesus Christ, that whoever believes in Him, shall not perish but have everlasting life![85]"

"Now explain the greatest word, please" said the Lord.

The angel understood the meaning of this answer from passing with great merits his class of Salvation 101 while beginning his testimony in the lower chambers of Heaven when he was just newly found. This angel said to his Creator, Master in Heaven, of whom he was fortunate to be his newest indentured

---
[82] I Corinthians 5:7, 11:3, 12:27,15:3, 15:14, 15:22,15:57,
[83] Luke 10: 27
[84] Luke 10:28
[85] John 3:16

slave[86], "To receive Eternal Life[87] one must believe[88] in Christ. To have true faith one must believe[89] in Christ. In order to have true love, one must believe[90] in Christ. To be truly loyal in service one must believe[91] in Christ, and to have true hope one must believe[92] in Christ. To have true trust[93] one must believe in Christ. And, to truly live[94] and have life abundantly[95] one must truly believe first[96] in Christ, for without belief, there is no hint of life.[97] The human word Believe truly means 'By-Life" and to see and understand what a man truly believes in his heart,[98] one must look at and judge the ways of his "Life". All the things he does,[99] says,[100] thinks,[101] and makes[102] will be written down in either the Book of Life[103] or Death[104]. If he is true to his word, and keeps his oaths and covenants, and true to his pledge(s), and true to his path which is given to him, then he is true to his belief, and he will honor his creator. If he is not true to his word, nor keeps his oaths and covenants, nor true to his pledge(s), nor true to the path which his creator has given to him then he truly does not believe, and he does not honor his creator. So, for all things, according to

---

[86] Titus 3:7
[87] John 3:15
[88] Luke 5:20S
[89] John 13:34
[90] John 14:15
[91] Matthew 20:26, 23:11
[92] Colossians 1:27
[93] Colossians 2:6-8
[94] Matthew 4:4
[95] John 10:10
[96] Mark 5:36
[97] Mark 5:41
[98] Mark 12:33, Matthew 6:21
[99] Galatians 6:4, 6:7-10
[100] Matthew 15:11
[101] Galatians 6:3
[102] John 6:27
[103] Revelation 3:5,13:8,17:8,20:12,21:27
[104] Revelation 20:15

the Father in Heaven and inheriting Eternal Life, they hinge on one thing, the greatest of all the mankind's words: 'Believe'[105]. For when a man says "I truly Believe (and he truly does), then this man and his life will reflect the true beliefs, and he shall then do, act, speak, and make ALL things with reverence[106] to his Lord, the Creator, which then truly reflects[107] his possession of treasure[108] in Heaven. And from that moment till the end of time… in the two worlds of Lower Paradise and also in upper Paradise, his fate now receive the ring of eternal life; just as his life will stand true in the Light[109], and clearly show what he truly believes, and also create a single legacy[110] which will be left to show others who also believe, The Way.[111]"

---

[105] John 8:23-24
[106] 2 Corinthians 7:1
[107] 2 Corinthians 3:18
[108] I Timothy 6:19
[109] Luke 8:16-17
[110] Luke 8:18
[111] John 14:6

-- Book of Parables III --

Divine Lesson #39

The First Right of all Rights

An angel came to the Lord and said, "I have heard the people walking amongst themselves. They are grumbling, gathering together to petition You for more rights... Is this wrong? I have heard you speak only of the rights of Heaven. What things do these men speak of?"

Then the Lord answered the angel with these words, tell them: "He who has an ear, let him hear what the Spirit says to the churches. To him who overcomes, I will give the *right* to eat from the tree of life, which is in the paradise of God."[112]

"But if you do not do what is *right*, sin is crouching at your door; it desires to have you, but you must master it.[113] So, if you know that Christ is the only *righteous* one, you know that anyone who does *right* will be born of him.[114] And to the one who overcomes I give the *right* to sit with Me on My throne, just as I overcame and sat down with My Father on His throne. He who has an ear let him hear what the Spirit says to the churches. [115]

---

[112] Revelation 2:7
[113] Genesis 4:7
[114] I John 2:26
[115] Revelation 3:21

-- Brian Smith --

Divine Lesson #40

Pompous-Ass Mercury

When the angel looked down on certain lost ones of mankind, he reported what he saw to God The Father in Heaven. He said of these they have a keen interest of listening to only opinion-based hyperbole of non-facts and inuendo[116], basking in self-indulged power[117], using the tools of political spin using character assassination[118], and laughing amongst themselves in unholy misguided humor[119], all without praying for divine wisdom or forgiveness first[120]. Then the angel asked the Lord, "Why is Man was so eager to trade his most valuable possession, his very short-allotted time to write his eternal well-being, for so much doomsday irreverence of You and eternal suffering?"[121]

So, the Lord said, "Bring Me a golden lyre, a silver flute, and a platinum drum all for the angels to play on this day in Hades[122], and I will give you're your answer with Holy enlightenment."

---

[116] John 8:44
[117] Job 21:7, Ecclesiastes 4:1
[118] Exodus 20:16, Matthew 26:59
[119] Proverbs 29:9
[120] James 1:5
[121] I Corinthians 1:19, Proverbs 8:5
[122] Revelation 1:18

So, Michael and his angels under him, did as they were commanded,[123] and the Lord God said, "Play these instruments to Me one a time, and play them over the lost soul of those who prayed to Hermes[124], to see what he does as he listens in his grave."

So, the angels went to the gravesites of the dead and did as the Lord asked. They played each of them and reported to the Lord these things… They said to Him, "when we played the golden lyre above Hermes, we saw his aching soul change colors from dark to light, then he moved a bit, but not much. When we played the silver flute over him, Hermes began to dance inclined and staying down by himself because had no-other to dance with. He stopped and started again and again then he just laid still. And when we played the platinum drum over him, he rose up from his grave for a short time, as did all the other lost souls around him and they all began to march in unison up and down the streets of the entire graveyard as Hermes got into a long line somewhere in the middle which became a parade for the lost after which they promptly returned each to their graves once the drum stopped beating its sound."

"You are correct… oh, wise observers, My Watchers"[125], the Lord said to His angels, and then Lord turned and began to leave from them, going back to His business of protecting Lower Paradise from Satan's untruths.[126]

When the angels saw this of Him, they asked, "Oh great Creator of the Universe[127], Ruler over both the living and the

---

[123] Matthew 4:6
[124] Acts 14
[125] Daniel 4:17
[126] Mark 8:33
[127] Isaiah 40:28

Dead[128], will you tell us this, to all of your servant angels about You, why You design these things to happen in this way?"

The Lord stopped! Then He turned back around and said to all those who had gathered round His feet in that instant, "If man is to be truly loved by Me, and be separated part of the dirt from which He once came, his soul must be awaken from its sleep,[129] and only I can wake him with the sound of My voice calling Him,[130] like a lyre which has many strings from which I will play to him. After he is awakened, he will look for someone to dance with because he was not created to be alone and if he does not find Me knocking at his door[131], he will return to his grave, to lie again once more still in eternity in the ground from which he was created.[132] But If I beat my drum loud enough so they all can hear Me, all good Men will get up as dead men walking[133] and they will follow each other, and those who are unable to hear My voice,[134] they will march to a beat that will lead them back to their graves after their short commute, and all those who once could move around freely by their own will are now unable to move at all[135], as you my angels in Heaven can now."

Then the Lord God opened the minds of those who were listening then and said unto them, "The graveyards are vast arenas of fertile dead mortal ground, ready to be filled with both the bones of the believers and non-believers, as they lie in huge circles, endless in all directions, and limitless down beyond your

---

[128] Revelation 20:13
[129] John 11:11, Romans 13:11 John 5:28-29
[130] John 11:25, 11:43-44
[131] John 10:7-9
[132] Jeremiah 18
[133] Romans 6
[134] John 9:31
[135] Matthew 7:26

feet. Hermes came and went on his own free time and own free will, but I knew him naught. He spent his life worshipping and storing up temporary mercurial things[136] he thought were good[137] and which made him happy, but he is never happy again. I gave him wings on his feet to run like the wind, but to my angels I gave them bigger wings on their shoulders so they could rise above him, shadowing him as Hermes chose to stay on the ground, and communicate only with those on the ground; and then later, be in the ground. There he shall stay just as he was in his beginning, and with all those who chose the same earthly temporary fame, fortune, glory, riches and their eternal dirt over me.[138] For in the end, in all man's affairs seeking hard to own more of what he is rightfully given, the total amount of dirt he is to gain is only enough to cover his bones in the ground; and even that dirt I eternally own because I created it also and I will not return it to him for a second life…So, let those hear who can hear, listen and hear…For the man who always believes he knows the most, smirking in his arrogance[139] and pride[140]: he who is pompous and haughty[141], who believes there is no final judgement waiting for him or anyone which is still yet to be judged[142]…this is of the group if unbelievers who is most to be pitied and never unborn.[143]"

---

[136] Matthew 6:20
[137] Hebrews 5:14
[138] Matthew 10:38
[139] James 4:16
[140] Proverbs 16:18
[141] 2 Timothy 3:2
[142] Matthew 25:31-46
[143] Revelation 20:15

-- Brian Smith --

The Only Standard

An angel went to the Lord and asked Him, "By what standard must a man or woman live to enter the Kingdom of Heaven?"[144]

"Only by My Standard, not man's; and not by any other,[145]" says the Lord.

Then the angel asks, "Can you tell me, is Your standard written down[146], taught[147], inspired[148], or transformed[149]? Is it invisible[150], or visible[151]? Does it cling to the lips of prophets[152], or said on the last breath of thieves[153]? Or live more in the minds [154]of men, or more in the hearts[155] of saints?"

---

[144] Matthew 19:16, Deuteronomy 5, Matthew 5:20
[145] Matthew 19:18, 19:21,5:48, 19:23
[146] Luke 24:44
[147] John 3:2
[148] I Thessalonians 1:3
[149] Romans 12:2, 2 Corinthians 3:18
[150] Colossians 1:15
[151] Colossians 1:16
[152] Matthew 22:40, Luke 24:25, Romans 3:21
[153] Luke 23:40-43
[154] Hebrews 8:10, 10;16, Luke 24:45, Ephesians 4:23, Colossians 3:2
[155] Philemon :7, II Corinthians 1:22, 3:2-3, 4:6, 6:11, Galatian 4:6, Ephesians 3:17

"All of the above, because I have given it all to man first through My love,[156]" said the Lord.

"How can it this be? Is not one part of each of these exclusive of the other, disqualifying (divorcing them) from the whole?[157]" said the angel.

Then the Lord said, "No![158] My Standard is always the same: open and inclusive, never closed and exclusive. I sent my Son to show all men who are born of the womb of man, The Standard Way... He is The Risen[159] The Standard,[160] The Bearer of Truth[161], The Light of the world that shines in the darkness[162], and The Way[163]; and no other Standard either written, worshipped, followed is worthy of Me[164]. Christ is My beloved Son (My Standard), and in Him I am well-pleased[165]. His words came as invisible in the beginning[166], then made visible in life[167] to be fruitful in the hearts of all men[168]; to make all saints Holy[169] and have pure hearts[170], bound only by love[171], grace[172], and mercy[173] tempered with loyal obedience[174]. Without

---

[156] John 3:16
[157] Malachi 2:16
[158] Matthew 7:7-8, Revelation 3:20
[159] Matthew 167
[160] Job 19:25,
[161] John 14:6
[162] John 8:12
[163] John 14:6
[164] Matthew 7:21
[165] Matthew 3:17
[166] John 1;1
[167] John 1:14
[168] Deuteronomy 11:18, Psalms 119: 11
[169] I Peter 1:15, Hebrews 10:10
[170] Philemon :7
[171] Romans 8:35
[172] Romans 6:14
[173] Romans 11:32
[174] Ephesians 6:8

following Him[175], and taking up His path[176], which he walked to Calvary[177] as My standard, all men will fall short[178]. To seek any other's path of man's journey without first shouldering His cross[179] and receiving My enlightenment[180] by The Standard of The Christ, is folly. I tell you the truth, no one shall enter the Kingdom of Heaven lest they follow the name and blood sacrifice of the Son[181] in whom I am well pleased[182]. He is the Standard, the prophesied one. His name is Jesus and He is The Standard, the only name which rises above other names in the kingdom of Heaven.[183] Without Jesus, all will fail and also fall short of the Kingdom[184], not receiving My standard to enter.[185]"

---

[175] John 14:6
[176] Ephesians 3:7-11
[177] Matthew 16:24
[178] Matthew 5:22
[179] Luke 14:27, Mark 8:34
[180] Hebrews 6:4
[181] Hebrews 9:15
[182] Philippians 2:8-11
[183] I John 1:8
[184] Luke 12:5
[185] Romans 3:23

-- Book of Parables III --

Divine Lesson #42

If You Love Me

An angel of the Lord went to the God The Father and said, "You have commanded me to be Your messenger of Your will, while also shedding light on man's errors, while being faithful to The Holy Spirit, and led by the Truth of Jesus[186],....So, how then does an angel like me best communicate the words of God speaking the words of man, so that all might understand the right ways of hearing?"

God The Father responded saying, "This thing you ask is an easy thing. You must begin each sentence you speak while being in prayer with these four words…If you love me."

Then the angel said, "This I understand. I will."

The Lord God then in unison repeated again saying, "Truly, I tell you, you must begin each sentence with every choice they struggle with to begin with these four words: If you love me (or because you love Me) and the Holy Spirit will handle all the rest…"

And what if they ask again, because they do not understand, the first time? Said the angel.

---

[186] John 14: 6

"Then you tell them, these words, "Fear Not! ... If you love Me, you will do these things, and Because You love Me, you will understand... For My words were affirmed by the life of My Son (which He them said well), as did the the prophets and the apostles, which all affirmed...

"If you love Me, you will keep My commandments..."[187]

"If you love Me, thou shall not have any other Gods before Me."[188]

If you love Me, thou shalt not commit adultery."[189]

"If you love Me, thou shalt not use My name in vain."[190]

"If you love Me, thou shalt not murder."[191]

"If you love Me, thou shalt honor thy mother and father."[192]

"If you love Me, though shalt not bear false witness."[193]

"If you love Me, thou shalt not be prideful."[194]

"If you love Me, thou shalt not covet thy neighbor's wife, or anything which belongs to thy neighbor."[195]

"If you love Me, thou shalt feed My lambs."[196]

---

[187] John 14:15
[188] Deuteronomy 5:7
[189] Deuteronomy 5:18
[190] Deuteronomy 5:11
[191] Deuteronomy 5:17
[192] Deuteronomy 5:16
[193] Deuteronomy 5:20
[194] Philippians 2:3
[195] Deuteronomy 5:21
[196] John 21: 15-17

"If you love Me, thou shalt not lead others astray."[197]

"If you love Me, thou shalt observe and keep the Sabbath holy."[198]

"If you love Me, thou shalt not bow down to any image."[199]

"If you love Me, thou shalt not think impure thoughts."[200]

"If you love Me, thou shalt heal the sick, raise the dead, cleanse those of infection, and drive out demons."[201]

"If you love Me, thou shalt not listen nor follow false prophets."[202]

"If you love Me, thou shalt not steal."[203]

"If you love Me, thou shalt love thy neighbor as thy self."[204]

"If you love Me, thou shalt be eager to listen and slow to speak."[205]

"If you love Me, thou shalt be eager to be by My side."[206]

"If you love Me, thou shalt not judge."[207]

---

[197] Romans 14:13-23, Matthew 18:6
[198] Deuteronomy 5:12
[199] Deuteronomy 5:8
[200] Hebrews 4: 12-13
[201] Matthew 10:8
[202] Matthew 7:15-20
[203] Deuteronomy 10:4
[204] Matthew 22:39
[205] James 1:9
[206] 2 Timothy 4:17
[207] Luke 6:37

"If you love Me, thou shalt not harm Thyself."[208]

"If you love Me, thou shall stay out of the courts of man."[209]

If you love Me, thou shalt love and cherish your spouse."[210]

"If you love Me, thou shalt run from sin and all thoughts of sinfulness."[211]

[212]If you love Me, thou shalt fear Me."

"If you love me, thou shalt not worry."[213]

"If you love Me, thou shalt do no harm to the world nor thy neighbor, both of which I created."[214]

"If you love Me, thou shalt let Me be thy God and follow Me in all my ways, not yours."[215]

"If You love Me, thou shalt give freely, just as you have you have received freely."[216]

"If you love Me, thou shalt forgive others, just as I have forgiven you."[217]

---

[208] Proverbs 8:36
[209] Matthew 5:25
[210] Ephesians 5:33
[211] Jeremiah 51:6
[212] Philippians 2:12, Acts 9:31
[213] Matthew 6:25
[214] Revelation 7:3, Romans 13:10
[215] John 14:10
[216] Matthew 10:8
[217] Matthew 6:15, Luke 6:37

"If you love Me, thou shalt use the gifts and talents I loan thee to honor the Kingdom of Heaven, and not honor the kingdom of thyself."[218]

"If you love me, you will give back to me a part of the first fruits I have loaned to thee, as a good steward of better things promised to come."[219]

"If you love Me, thou shalt not love an animal more than Me, or man."[220]

"If you Love Me, thou shalt not exasperate your children."[221]

"If you love Me, thou shalt pick up thy cross and follow Me."[222]

"If you love Me, wives shalt not abandon their husbands if they are unbelievers."[223]

"If you love me, thou shalt also love thy enemies, and do good to them."[224]

"If you love Me, thou shalt also obey what I command."[225]

"If you love Me, thou shalt also love one another as you love yourself."[226]

---

[218] Revelation 4:11
[219] Proverbs 3:9-10
[220] Matthew 10:37
[221] Colossians 3:21
[222] Matthew 10:38
[223] I Corinthians 7:13-14
[224] Luke 6:27, Luke 6:35
[225] John 14:15
[226] John 15:12, John 15:17

"If you love Me, thou shalt do everything in love."[227]

"If you love Me, thou shalt bear one another in love."[228]

"If you love Me, thou shalt love you wives, just as I love the church."[229]

"If you love Me, thou shalt not love money."[230]

"If you love Me, thou shalt love each other deeply."[231]

"If you love Me, thou shalt not love the world or anything in it."[232]

"If you love Me, thou shalt not fear anything but Me."[233]

"If you love Me, thou shalt walk in love, truth, and obedience."[234]

"If you love Me, thou shalt not envy."[235]

"If you love Me, thou shalt not provoke." [236]

"If you love Me, thou shalt not be conceited."[237]

"If you love Me, thou shalt do good to all people; especially to the Family of Believers." [238]

---

[227] I Corinthians 16:14
[228] Ephesians 4:2
[229] Ephesians 5:25
[230] I Timothy 6:10
[231] I Peter 1:22, 4:8
[232] I John 2:15
[233] I John 4:18
[234] 2 John :5-6
[235] Galatians 5:26
[236] Galatians 5:26
[237] Galatians 5:26
[238] Galatians 6:10

"If you love Me, thou shalt not slander."[239]

"If you love Me, thou shalt give back to Me first fruits of thy labor."[240]

"If you love Me, thou shalt not engage in incest, bestiality, or sexual morality."[241]

"If you love Me, thou shalt not deceive."[242]

"If you love Me, thou shalt not be lewd."[243]

"If you love Me, thou shalt not hate God."[244]

"If you love Me, thou shalt not be boastful."[245]

"If you love Me, thou shalt not have haughty eyes and a proud heart."[246]

"If you love Me, thou shalt submit to Thy Father's will."[247]

"If you love Me, thou shalt remember My Son by Eating of his flesh and drinking of His blood, whereby then being in holy communion with Me."[248]

"If you Love Me, thou shalt not allow women to lead My churches."[249]

---

[239] Leviticus 19:16, Matthew 15:19
[240] Ezekiel 44:30
[241] I Corinthians 5:1
[242] Mark 7:22
[243] Mark 7:22
[244] Romans 1:30
[245] Romans 1:30
[246] Psalm 101:5
[247] Hebrews 13:17, James 4:7
[248] John 6:53-55
[249] I Corinthians 14:34-35

"If you love Me, thou shalt not make excuses for man's wickedness to suppress the truth."[250]

"If you love me, thou shalt not let sin reign in your mortal body so that you obey its evil desires, nor offer the parts of your body to sin."[251]

"If you love Me, though shalt not gamble."[252]

---

[250] Romans 1: 18-20
[251] Romans 6:12-13
[252] Hebrews 13:5, Luke 12:15

www.ingramcontent.com/pod-product-compliance
Lightning Source LLC
Chambersburg PA
CBHW041756040426
42446CB00001B/54